LIFELINES

ALSO BY ROBIN MAGOWAN

Internal Weather
The Rim of Dawn
Improbable Journeys
Memoirs of a Minotaur
Lilac Cigarette in a Wish Cathedral
America, America
New Wine
Fabled Cities of Central Asia
Narcissus and Orpheus
Kings of the Road
Tour de France
Sweets
Voyages

TRANSLATIONS

A Rose Garden of Persian Poetry
The Garden of Amazement: Scattered Gems after Saeb
Bidel, *The Mirrored Spectrum*
Verlaine, *Bordel*
Claudel, *100 Sentences Written Upon Fans*
Devrient, *Martini with a Splash of Dawn*
Michaux, *Ecuador*

LIFELINES

poems

ঌ

Robin Magowan

Story Line Press | Pasadena, CA

Book design by Mark E. Cull

Library of Congress Cataloging-in-Publication Data

Names: Magowan, Robin, author.
Title: Lifelines: poems / Robin Magowan.
Description: First edition. | Pasadena, CA: Story Line Press, 2023.
Identifiers: LCCN 2023018891 (print) | LCCN 2023018892 (ebook) | ISBN
    9781636281407 (paperback) | ISBN 9781636281414 (ebook)
Subjects: LCGFT: Poetry.
Classification: LCC PS3563.A3527 L54 2023 (print) | LCC PS3563.A3527
    (ebook) | DDC 811/.54—dc23/eng/20230425
LC record available at https://lccn.loc.gov/2023018891
LC ebook record available at https://lccn.loc.gov/2023018892

The National Endowment for the Arts, the Los Angeles County Arts Commission, the Ahmanson Foundation, the Dwight Stuart Youth Fund, the Max Factor Family Foundation, the Pasadena Tournament of Roses Foundation, the Pasadena Arts & Culture Commission and the City of Pasadena Cultural Affairs Division, the City of Los Angeles Department of Cultural Affairs, the Audrey & Sydney Irmas Charitable Foundation, the Meta & George Rosenberg Foundation, the Albert and Elaine Borchard Foundation, the Adams Family Foundation, Amazon Literary Partnership, the Sam Francis Foundation, and the Mara W. Breech Foundation partially support Red Hen Press.

First Edition
Published by Story Line Press
an imprint of Red Hen Press
www.redhen.org

for Juliet
and in memory of James Merrill

CONTENTS

I. Dawn Steps

II. Greece, Dancing

III. Sabering Light

IV. Abroad

V. Seasonal Substrate

VI. Intimacies

LIFELINES

I

DAWN STEPS

MAT-RIDING

I stand, green as that beginning
when wave first flowered into child and, mat
in hand, I ran to my white-capped home
out among the tumbling casks. Those waves
may not be the night, but they come crying
with night's full fire. It's their lit depths
I ride, hurtling onto foam, sand.

When they roll me, it's a lifetime ago:
fish swim in my eyes, pebbles scrape me red,
my head bounces off the bottom, stunned.
Gathering breath, I dive flatter than a shadow
until the whole train's length has thundered by.

Insanity glitters, "Crawled out of you,
wave, I'm crawling my way back
through the slits in the breaking wall."
I'm coming home, home where I once belonged.
Ahead a path opens, I must! I will!
Chin down, I hop on, flailing my way
out of the vast dissolute cathedral.

Black-crack-moonlight. I'm safe, floating
in the froth, feeling the wind behind
shadow, behind blade. Everything
is teeth, savage, distant. Mine are chattering.
I want nothing more than to be the arc
over that fire spume. To that end I wait
till a comber looms, frightening enough
to ride, "If not for this, why be out here?"
Spur to set me paddling. Then wave and I

collide as the mat jerks forward, barreling
me on a cushion of foam onto land.

MISE-EN-SCÈNE

In the ice of distance a sun shone.
Reptiles ran. Music
distended like a river, rippling.
Wind! Desserts! Cheese-
making equipment!
Wonders like socks and shoes
filled grass with their steps.

Later, between hills, lakes emerge,
smudges of blue, or brown, or black.
Soon in this rural mise-en-scène
investment's troops of corn,
potatoes, even mice,
would dot the next crowded bend
with their fruit tree friends.
Night fiends, too, proliferate,
poor-wills, slow-winged owls.

Not everyone is thrilled
when the first insect inspectors arrive.
Accusations flap like laundry
on lines criss-crossing into confusion.
That's me, prepared
to sit on a knot & not budge
until my rope has vanished
in a squad of electrocuted fireflies
and the sandwiches of silence
litter the ground.

THE MIND OF A TRAVELER

One can argue with fate
in its many guises
but it usually comes back

to sitting. I, for sanity,
have to keep shuffling
these feet about, devotee

of elsewhere, even if only
in the land of another
clutching a theoretical sky.

Driven by something—
an internal temperature?—
I mosey back, forth,

never arriving, while wind
in its cast-iron sleeves
watches, bemused.

Is silence the one adversary
before whom any truce
can only be provisional?

Am I to believe the sun
inadvertently slowed down
on the far side of the view?

How would that articulate?
I want a certain particular
that is my fate

alone in a white dress
to step off the boat
and rush up the landing

where it always snows
where pencils are on fire
in the snow.

SEVEN, WITHOUT BINOCULARS

Beaks, flashing plumages, feminine
cries, an illumined immensity
      shatters as I
crawl into the tick and bramble-
infested next door lot. Is this child
      oaf a new make
of bulldozer? A need to somehow
atone conjures me onto a log:
      a breathing stone,
unscribbled bark. When invisible
moss has grown over my face, and eyes
      are shivering
ice on a thin staring pole, I start
edging my way forward, a dime in
      a vase of wind.
My shadow sticks, my breath, a hushed mouth-
open, points at a silhouette, size
      of a nugget,
agleam in a far crown. Without lenses
how notice the telltale flash as she
      twitters and calls?
By becoming myself a bird!
I too plummet from leaf to song-
      lit life. Nowhere
to go, but up! flat on my back
scanning treetops for warbler eye stripes.
      "In my next life
let me be you, flitting syllable,
only stay put until I've named you."
      Is that the gold
my wings glisten with, as if craning

a degree more, I'd no longer be
  this robin-named
boy, but new ore, bent on a bough.

DANCING SCHOOL

"Only sissies like girls!" Yet there I was
packed into dress shirt, tie, blazer
and bundled off to a ballroom's nymphs
in their unsettling blouses, flaring skirts.
I was far from adept at the box step
I had to convert to a fluency
as if the quick-quick-slow of the fox trot
were a wave and there on its crest, palm
firmly ensconced in the small of her back,
were the two of us gliding ever so slightly
ahead of the looming beat. The formal box,
constricting at first, conferred a freedom
in which all illusions, even flight's double-
winged circling, stood encouraged. Sentenced
to a boy's exclusive plane—forward!—
I was discovering the leverage
to sail out past the surrounding traffic
a girl's stepping backward offered,
as did swaying between the two, neither
of us knowing what would occur next,
but balanced, with each other, ready.

BROLGA CRANES, DANCING

For days, along the Bensbach, we've watched
their pas de deux, step by synchronous
step, stately gliding. From miles away
their trumpeting insinuates our dawn.

In a flooded shale, one noon, we spot
two hundred of their beleaguered sect.
Single file, we tiptoe to a stand
of casuarinas. How peacefully
they browse, well over four feet tall, gray
with rust crowns and red-striped beaks. All
of a sudden a crown lifts, wings fan out,
bouncing as if on stilts, like linen
blown about in a gale. A second
crane rises, addresses her. Wingtips
spreading like petals, the two lift
and bounce down. Now, facing each other,
they take the air in the dream of flight
we call dancing, wingwork suspended,
yet afloat, as if the air held a rhythm
sustaining where their feathered selves touch,
teetering, before side-slipping down.
Never more than a house high, the two
leap, flapping. Life mates now, they fly away
to enact what their wings have whispered.

BIRTH

I

Light speckles the hospital wall
as day like a grove of oranges
begins to dawn. Attendants
drift in & out, nothing can be done,
nothing that won't stop you.
Sixteen hours later you strike
the screams
sing
and dusk
is cut in sandwiches
of green & gold. Threads
wind out of your eyes
where you lie stretched
across her belly's amber
as in a vial of oil
mouth wide & twisted like a harp
eyes the color of
distant firs & mountains
corners tilting up like small pontoons.

II

Behind your nursery glass
mittened hands stir
in tide pool sleep, starfish
searching, and blind-
eyed you wade
seeking your length of gum-
green water like the answer
to some dream of distant raft
and sunlight,
thistle & thigh-white cloud.

FIR-SCENTED RAIN

Rain, long-
toothed comb coats and subdues.
The senses breathe, cobra-
headed grebes floating on their disks
beaks outstretched
gathering the glisten where the moon is salt.
They dive down a legend of fishes.
Islands plunge past,
shot with silk and the mahoganies of silence
tall once, but so long borne in the cycles of water
only crests remain
and these too threatening to dissolve into the moss
of a forest that's also a vast tenement:
conifers growing out of other conifers
and others, waiting in line,
with the uptilted faces of would-be stars.
Trees so numerous the painter ends
by replacing them with woodpeckers.
In the fire of their beaks I move,
creating a void I fill with their tiny needles
of fir-scented rain.

BERKELEY, 1967

From that first Gathering of the Tribes
flows a wave on which each of our rafts
is caught and lifted, melted, molded.
Tomorrow's cut glass. In a single week
all the bras in town vanish. Flag-
striped asses swagger by, showing how
I could crawl out on a limb and, with a shout,
a barbaric yawp, go all the way.
An instantaneous transformation,
of both myself and the entire planet,
viewed from that bend of the Yellow Brick Road,
looks just out of sight, a horizon away.

Join us, the Be-In urged, make love, not war.
Well, not everyone can be embraced.
As the backlash set in, a pot
and psychedelic-powered culture fell
prey to understandable paranoia.
At concerts no one danced any more, we sat.
Kids no longer greeted their narcs
with cookies and yogurt, but booby traps.
Out went PEACE and LOVE and in came ACTION
roaring bats in hand through our classes
controlled—egged on?—by squadrons
of visor-helmeted, mace-throwing Blue Meanies
directed from Nam-style, spy-in-the-sky copters.
The war had, with a vengeance, come home.

HISTORIC DISTRICT, CHARLESTON

Can I be the only one to have stumbled into the wrong century?
Less excluded, perhaps, than pushed aside, gently. Bougainvillea,
stippling a walled lane, keeps intact the whiff of something rotten:
the smoke of defeat and slavery, the fragrance of death; a stench
brought back to more than ephemeral life. These brick
and azalea-draped alleys speak with an eloquence I somehow trust.

I don't stroll so much as come again and again to a pause.
Rather than proceed, I would rather dig down into a world
where each doorway offers an opening rooted in the humid
extravagance of skin and sense and smell. Why make of
difference something other than a breath unlocked? Are
we all only intermittently of our time?

The late afternoon narrows, grows calm as I cross a cobbled
lane and hop aboard a last conveyance.

ESCARPMENT

on still grassy heights

(where a good-
sized hive
of cliff
people thrived)

questions
and quiet

cracked tables

held together
by wind

II

GREECE, DANCING

SHEPHERDS

after Claude

Watching them in that thin morning
of the world, I note less the sheep
or temples than the threads of light
binding them to flutes, the echoing
ravines and, secretly, one another.
Day becomes opaline. Their earth
is not only olive, salt, wine,
but the echo and response
of birds, pasture, trees,
the clarity of unblemished distance.

SAILORS AT PÉREMA

Fingers snapping, the two move
circling, as on the rim of a glass:
palms, soft-spinning flowers;
feet, spokes in a cycle of prayers.
They speak in a tongue of rain
sensing through the jukebox's din
hands all around
breaking in green time like plates.

NOON TAVERNA

Secrecies of air—
wine and flies

PAROS

Across the bay, beyond where the sea,
a giant crab, pinches in, hills rise
seemingly immense beneath their crust
of morning shadow. Fields ripple out, tiers
of green and gold speckled with poppies—
as many poppies as stalks of wheat—
perhaps in a corner the white legato
of a farm binds fields and sea.

The eye shears downwards past blue-domed farms,
all terrace, with steps like lumps of sugar,
to where in a pot of flame the sea
funnels the light's last oils, the farms
reaching their whitewash down to it
like tongues and up, over the cobbles,
drawing it skywards, like a first breath.

The sea's bitter smoke holds the eyes
of the fishermen, content to sit
before huge glasses and simply stare,
holds the singer's voice, high, honeylike,
reaching over the bay with the flat
even insistency of a serpent
over grass, until a fisherman
rises—hissing—from his table,
his arm a mast, moving in a vortex
over the floor, eyes down, the slow circles
descending, searching, the sea with him
naming her, the sound a thread downwards
through the spool of hisses guiding as
he steers over its tilting sun-dialed frame

and light pours its daggers into him, melting
the streets into a wax, while the head, dis-
membered, floats out over the singing stones.

TAPESTRY

Midday's olive trees salaam
beaded blues,
grays, fountaining
over a tinder of bright
basket yellows stitched
thick with horses, goats
fig trees, small rooster-
colored houses,
under an oak the bell
of a herd boy, crumpled.
The hours wait, unseen, heavy.
Only blueness, a far
harbor writhing, oyster
in the still
pointed sun.

THE PAINTER

for Aristodimos Kaldis

Olympus
rises out of paper
capped with brows
of curling juniper. Each
touch marks an explosion
of cypress & thumb-
pressed olive trees,
against which the red
& blue house stands
atilt in a splatter of lime-
hued steps.
In the noon silence the breath
of a broom swings,
swings & becomes sail, a bay
full of kelp, bathing suits, laughter.

The mountain rides,
afloat in a dream of lava,
slopes gathering meadows
poppy-singed
where only the breadth
of a cypress sways
& invisible
among almonds
a ploughman whistles.

ZEMBEIKIKO

An old peasant gets up   turns
takes   steps on   makes with his hands
fuse of a cigarette   crackle   sing
In the ash of his glass   dancing
the floor   a round white   over which he stoops
hops twice   JUMPS!
sizzle of browns
blacks   flash
of a horsewhip
stubble-bright falling

Z

Zembeikiko
Says it! His is
hisses! He takes something round
shape of a palm and with it
hits / smashes: floor trousers   shoes
scoops   slices   spins
Is manna is hands is sunwhip & stone
is the man who says   NO I'M NOT
old Coocoocooroooo
who suncaps shoes & washes the stones
in the verminous oxides of night
& stands   tongue of crow   floorblack hands shouting

I HANDS RAIN COME
LOOKING FOR YOU DADDY
WHO GAVE ME THIS NAME WORM
A giant fist dances sings
shoes plates hair glittering phosphorescent shirts
through which he mosquito-bright glides
white   dipping
moving all over the floor

              moving
              sowing
              threshing
I am me   he says   I burn the knife I cry

Wings soar & melt
The fire
is the globe I am

ZAGORIANA

I

Day: the milk in a bowl
of glass is born.

I have only to separate hands
from face to begin to see:

a blackness of pink erasers, notes
called forth like trousers from the mist.

Clefs of harebells stripe sunlit cliffs
where dwellings cling, range

upon echoing range, where hamlets
gleam like far-off candles

and stroke-crowned vistas dissolve
in a mass of smoldering buttercups,

the snow of an exclamation—
one jagged insult upon the next—

that challenge the wind
with upright possibilities.

II

Evening: high on the mountainside
dancers like falcons

(faces burnt, moustached,
only the hooded eyes gleam)

glide as on a current, slow,
falling back three paces,

then swaying forward.
Since life's what no one owns

they must not be afraid to throw themselves
out on the wind. A stamp

defines the signal,
issuing as from a single throat

that pencils them on the air.
Anchored in wind, they are

the smoke of summer, match-
quick fingers, lightning vests.

Men cherish the honor
that rides on the knife belt

seeking the one route
open to the sky.

CYTHERA

The island
turns in its noon indigo
its air swimming
Shadows lie in knife-bright trance
I want not one stone
removed   not one lizard

A frantic hold of shallows
cards like caïques slapping a table
The forks speak
the donkey rags go home
only I am left
cup in a mouth of sunlight

III

SABERING LIGHT

DEATH VALLEY CAMPGROUND

I hear noises gathering, sorrows
being leashed, as if the bumpity-bump-
bump of the train to sleep
were nothing more than a tent's chattering
praying for a kinder hour.
Then from the witch inside comes a leaden rattle—
my own death riding high?
rattling as sometimes train wheels rattle
creaking through the long desert.
Will I stumble my way there, head
tossing now to one side, now the other,
measuring the sun by the rays it expressly
lets fall? What if my lips, too,
were a sun washing their shadows in salt,
their moon in convulsions,
heart for whom there are moments of you and I
tethered to the dream salt
necks bowed and like horses drinking.
I am the head I fold these ropes over,
you, Love, the bitterness I must expunge
because who needs another sun
wringing him to his own tent, own skin?

CRUCIBLE

Buoyed by a half-pie of grass,
by the magnets of her breasts
glowing through their tank top,
I join her on the trailer floor,
paw seeking out the "That's so good,
man!" moans, while as from a wall
away, her smoker's croak-shadow
voice responds, fire in a throat.
Into that blaze I strike, the raven-
black mane in whose thick pelt
probing fingers luxuriate,
each lock a prospective serpent
to tie to my own risen mount
until, a serpent now myself,
head swinging to her twining legs'
shoulder-propped censer, I plunge
where screams hammer and dreams sing.

MESCALINE HOPSCOTCH

O joy, jumping up with lead
o joy, mounting all my veins
to cobra a forest, cigarette ash my brains
o joy, o joy, neon-crimson cigarettes
o joy, o joy, jumping up in smoke
o joy, o joy, hooks in-finite
o joy, o joy, jumping matchstick cigars
o joy, o joy, jumping funeral parlors
o joy, o joy, anything you can imagine
o joy, o joy, I-I-I cannot
o joy, o joy, jump any longer
o joy, o joy, to the end of my rope
o joy, o joy, jumping out of the moon
o joy, o joy, what will it all come to?
o joy, o joy, how can it all go on?
o joy, o joy, jumping, jumping
o joy, o joy, jumping funeral parlors
jumping all along my mind
jumping, jumping,
jumping funeral parlors

ELEGY

The junk store. She waits outside
her Band-Aid box of a home.
He steps in. She pours a sandwich,
two nail slivers in one fried cream.
She has ghosts. She wants him to wait
because the ghosts aren't out yet.
She's afraid he'll go away.
People are such mice around her.
No, not eat them, just wash them
in her jelly until good and round
and hope someone arrives to light
up her door of incense and smiles.
She is Miss Hope in her Rothko dress
she tells herself, but even this wears thin.
Who now is her mirror talking to,
her lost life in the flaming dusk
stepping out of the car, seeing him,
saying "Hi!" in her flip-willow voice
and retiring to await whatever
might rebound? Motel where the two
stayed all of a week? The witnesses
were soft-spoken then, brought picnics
in rose baskets, looked under knees
and skirt for the flower tucked,
never the same, precious few
lately, she thinks, reminded
of the whipcord she used climbing,
plugging in where feet wouldn't grip
and hanging serenely for hours.
Later her home was Black Jock Rock.
Life there seemed more open, less full

of clothespins, she could have her way
without having to pay in paisley
sheets and doubled curlers: be
the brick by your side you desired.
I did. We shacked up down the hill
from Black Rock. Nights were cold there,
hips flared behind a pastry
she'd be fingering as she whispered
excitedly for me to come, try
some. We got fat together.
Lawns became lines we didn't mow.
Sleep-drenched mornings, when the duck
came out of her face and quacked,
evenings when we sat by a larch
and the honey dripped over our hands
and our voices came out like stars
and we shone back & forth as she
saw-pressed her hips up and I
burst in, like a sun in a fern
forest, and close-shouldered drank.
I drank her days of clear silver,
her wants with ropes in their claws,
her tongue, a kettle about my lit
sides. Young, I want to press
my toes up against her grains,
thin arms, mad sugarbush hair
where I enter—or don't, linger
in that last pool before the break
ensures disaster: plummeting finger-
stones, plummeting waterfall
of the green, green-gold eyes

holding self to a nether world
while one more open umbrellas
stories of starving fingers, storm-
worn hands, a few months passed
in a richness of uncommon thread.

IV

ABROAD

PAGODA

As under a vast squatting woman
the pilgrim sprawls, hands pointed,
touching, drumming.
Seven flights up, amid pennants,
a gold scepter beckons.
Parrots fly in, monkeys scamper,
from beam supports a girdle of carved
gilt leaves and dog bodies jut,
inviting. Higher, roofs gleam,
nodules quiver, each nod
of a head. Bell twanged,
prayer cask rotated,
what matter! Doesn't all matter
if life here above is the dream
of that other temple's
recumbent Vishnu, whale-
black on his ocean pad?

CHANG HOUSE

Coppery faces cupped by the wall bench.
Trays before them, mostly bare.
A black fire-stained peace.
The *chang* bowl is drunk, rinsed
and perhaps another tries its heron-
inscribed mist. No one talks.
Sweeping hands, wind-reddened faces.
From time to time a boy blows flute-like
into a grate where tea and potatoes steam.

I step out to a black so transparent
the quarter moon's enough
to light the lines of a path
mounting past farms and bare fields.
Everything seems to be waiting.

LILAC CIGARETTE IN A WISH CATHEDRAL

I

"Electric night,"
breathes who kneels
before a window unearthly
of moonbeam design
blue of hearts
and red of wine jousting
with enamel earrings
in cathedral
sun.

II

Checking out the allotment
the man kneels, beret
tipped to the valley floor,
taking in the wind
smearing the line of poplars
a sudden cadmium yellow
that leaves them shivering
silver in the monochrome of mud.

SCISSORS CUTTING PINES

I

The limits of smoke
and those of ice.
Of a great cloud in a white
sky.
Wind sailing the high seas of the Glass Bear.

II

Freeing solemnities:
winter, night, day.

III

Uncertainties pass.
In the morning there is jam,
blue from a crow, light it!
There comes a blackbird whistle
corkscrewing up to announce
a dark electric
in which the roof peaks
are giant fish tails, sailing.

IV

The chimney, aboil, stokes a pot.
Thermometers write away for sun.
I hold my wounds in my fingers
and they are taken away.

V

To a dream of boots in wind, feet stir
where an old stone bench mutes grounds
stuffed with struggling density.
"I am the tallest," "No, I am,"
argument in stalks, grasses, nettles.
Apple trees blossom, a few still so white!
and branches sway a myopic peace.
An unfinished project is a property
thousands of stones old, the stillness
forever lifting, like rain out of fog,
tempering my mist with quiets growing,
snails among blue bottles of periwinkle vine.

VI

Sitting, I feel able to turn any day
to a transparency that invites me
to look, to absorb. Only the texture
is perhaps too richly green.
Eventually I may go where the bustle
of moth and bird call is less, some cave
at the top of an arid valley where
"who am I" translates into a man
spun out of boots and rocks and sky.
For now, open as I am, the quickness
charms. I want to experience the long
leafy undressing as Burgundian blue
turns to copper envelope, mist sun,
wind's wonderful scissors cutting pines.

VI

Risen through the orchard
a moon husk to light my way,
I liberate myself from silences.
As I step I am.

BIRDS IN A FOREST, SWAYING

Belted Kingfisher

high on firepole
sentinel crest seething blue
a jazz monsieur
lights primary papers

Redwing Orchestra Afire

reeds'
black
red
& yellow-
winged
brasses

sticks
in holiday
blaze
strike up
demented
embers

Blue-crowned Motmot

a tiny fern
on exaggeratedly
stretched wings
flies into the far leafage
dangles
wind & rain-tossed

of everything liquid
the personal
blue
pronoun
sipping
      on uplifted
bough hot
sweet
green
air

Green Kingfisher

air, appareled,
penpoint, held
quivering, over a brook.

all lungs, I edge forward
eager to catch the roulade
of darting ink, green's
letter bearer.

Ruby-throated Woodstar

minuscule
the trill
that
as if
on strings
hangs

gorging
fastened
in the gauze
of an even less
visible
stalk

pointed neon-
blue tipped wings
a thumb-
beat long
flash a stark
tattoo
against
the gently

swaying
grassheads

Oncoming Rain

appetites quickened
ink-fired dots

dart
back & forth

soaking up
a skull-
black sky
they must forsake

for white
thinning
distinctions

Riverside Wren

white eye-stripe
red
tail-cocked
text
proclaims
sing yourself

and the riverside band
hurrahs ever more ebony blues
for you, father, whose feather
war pipe taught me to catch
woodnotes wild
before they detonate
dim late
to grass

KOAN

in the middle of
its bottle of moonlight
stands the crow

UNTITLED

carved out of sea mist
    the eagle's
        white head glows

V

SEASONAL SUBSTRATE

A PINPOINT OF SCARLET IN DVORAK

Bid the maple explode green
harmonies whose America
a tanager pinpoints, blaze
of sweets so fiery
only an incandescent-
stringed Iowa summer haze
could flatten it,
less a bird than a flutter
of migratory grace
black-winged on a score.

SUNSET

Painted into the parenthesis
between kiss and claws
a discreet music airs.
The agony of listening
subsides. Orange
distractions settle
hissing into the dusk.

In green silk
a messenger draws near.

SEPTEMBER

Among waves of apple trees
September bares its startling flute.

REMEMBER CROWS

Without the black
on blank
of a snowfield's crows

shifting
in the gust
like a fist-
ful of ripped leaves

what would November resemble?

NOVEMBER

How November strengthens the borders
of feeling: the digging in,

deep-rooted cellars, life
stooped, between blasts. Like a snake,

November shrugs off lost momentum,
coiled under blowing leaves at my feet.

November's enemy—the dazzling one, sun.
Between wet and dry, I'd vote

for water's shadowings, inexplicable
tears that disarrange the view.

And April's expansion,
spread shoulder, lifted lip.

DRIPPINGS

Things that make no sense
are dripping around me.

The music of appearance waits
in the snow's considered elegance.

Think fluffed feathers,
the rustle of vines.

A PLANT IN WINTER'S BED

Clothed in crystal fibers
I pursue erasure. Will light

kindle me to pry open the earth,
find its interred heart?

I may yet emerge
to life in the open

personal calligraphy
on the bowl I offer

persuaded I cannot be
other than what I am.

SCRIBBLINGS

Ice drips from the barn, transparencies
of twig and branch. I look
until what I'm seeing melts,
long lines of blue
scribbled across the whitest field.

RESONATING ROCK

I wake to crystal pocks on glass.
Notes balance on invisible spokes.

Only the unseasonal holds a pattern.
Untimely sleet

plagues the arrivals shed
where nursery plants

cower in trays
awaiting rock declivities.

The art, one of insertion.
I bury orchestral roots.

Is density, destiny,
infinity in a tiny room?

Only then, earthstrings
stretched taut, does the rockscape

resonate, sky and wind
struck into bloom.

INNUMERABLE BEES

Irresistible apples happen
                           because bees
rub their wings together.
May, blossoming, makes boughs
stretch their cups toward sky.
An inundation of blue! Papery
fragrances float over the lawn.

We walk under petals
unable to comprehend what prompts
the blue to risk such candor
or how an unremitting hum
shapes the shining grass, the round
thickenings of twigs, drenching
the distance.

PROCESSION

The path mounts to a meadow
where buttercups strut
and a cuckoo orchestrates the view.

Higher, pinnacled threads cling
to bodices afloat with dew.
Seedling belles

each from her lintel peering, pout
while insect inspectors debate
niceties of pollen,

shapes, stripes, cup size.
The thundering remorse of moss
staggers its remarks.

Now buds, unfolding, parade:
nodding bells, flamboyant
brasses, swirling reeds

swell briskly past
celebrating a garden's
brief affair with the sun.

CENTURY PLANT

Will I ever know what those spires
about to burst into tall
apoplectic gold
must feel?

VI

INTIMACIES

BETWEEN WAKE AND SLEEP

I

Blue as my bassinet the rowboat
floats all alone within a lake's fir-
touched transparencies. Looking up,
I become aware of a golden pathway,
corded like a harp, shimmering down.
Peering through shafts, I make out the far rungs
of an abandoned diving platform. At that
I feel held, a boat in a berceuse
of lapping wavelets, the summer crowd gone
and only a forest lake's coppery
cadences: quick leaves, wind shoulders, laughing.

II

This was the first hypnagogic image
I'd noticed. Now I looked for them. They rose
at some tide level between wake and sleep,
echoes of the woman beside me.
A man doesn't cross the gulf
to his primal waters on his own.

That left me the more beholden.
With what could I salute her?
From a word hoard I pluck "stocking," "shoe."
They combine in a boot, green, knee-high suede.
I set its green—in a lilac meadow!
Whereupon the boot once again morphs

into a meadow's wind-ruffled juniper.
Paging along the same rising meadow
I emerge onto a Pacific bluff
whose green shoulders are seen, up close,
to outline a frog, hunched, about to leap.
Onto? Following its gaze, I find,
inked against the blue, a tiny cypress.
How far! I marvel, how perfect! how soft!

III

Within her bush there glints a golden zone.
When her moon's propitious, I'm allowed
to leap, dancing a path into words
her welling fluids have set ablaze.
For a moment, maybe, I've engaged
with my chrysalis, I know by what lights
I sing, I dance, I weep. Then those blazing
convulsive seas recede and I'm left,
a moonless lake in the dead of night.

WIND CHANT

Wind curls around cliffs riding out tide
Wind curls through eyries—you'll go away I'll never see you
Wind curls under pines bringing wine   lice   hair
bringing a moose   oh how I love him
Wind dashes   slashes the rock levels
slops hair   wet   green   washes it down flip-flop
seal cry   toss of wave   oh how I love him
Wind curls in back of sea bone   among leaf boulders
where I stoop   wanting you to flavor me with your hand
wanting the long arrow   the cunning cleaning wound
wanting you to deliver me from eye
sound of eye on the wave glass
to clean my armpits of algae
to meadow my hair with red luck
to feast in my bed of bone and break it
hands over my wrists   mouth under my love car
oh how I love you   beast flapping wings over my embers
and I lighting up   meadow waves proudly
orange spume   come!   come!
breaking over me like rainbow salt
silvering the mist of my arms
granting me being   open as rain
blush in my bush of clouds

CHANTICLEER

That urge to spring
voice loud
inside his rusty lock

turn every chord
each lost
blue midnight key

to a vowel:
dawn-flushed
crimson-screaming O

NATURE MORTE

Stripped, incoherently
enlaced, his eye
notes how
in the black
tines
of a comb

parked
on a white
plate

a whole forest
on fire
roars.

MINIATURE

The pleasure of sounds innocently grasped.
A peacock in the eyes of the rain?

TONGUES

Thrust out of thick
glottal languishings

a thrashing labyrinth
sows seals salts
itself afresh:

oceans of wandering seamen

seedlings, alp-
licked, glowing

TO A MINIMALIST

I

If only your cubes of blue
or green
or red

could unblock
the wind
inherent in
seeing

II

Emptiness's blade
never quite suffices

so long as a sail
billowing
in a pair of lips

arrays a red
luminous orchestra.

ZAMBIAN BAR-GIRL

Beneath her hat's waterstar earrings
pond-shadowed eyes:
nose, a blunted mountain,
luminous;
hair braided in thatched rows;
silver bracelet, resonant
as the snap of a twig,
a thrush call;

skin, a slice
of thin water on polished stone,
whose mango shirt, accentuating palm,
makes her forearm's rose-
black skin glisten.

Her body breathes him in, glade
where the air hangs silver
and a pool, bubbling, becomes breast,
cones of a moon-drenched sheet.

NUPTIAL SUITE

sunlight
shatters

as grass is
born
     waist-
length locks
asleep

to founder
in the most wet
shining of
pools—
     like grass, she thinks,
horse, come

will the sun
that breathes on the door
of his being
be no more than these days
of skin and water
he lifts and drinks?

deep within her internal forest
she hears him exploding
the woods rocking
and the sperm flakes
one by one
floating down

where they lie, piled,
leg over rump, two
soft pink-
green

alligators

alligators

CONSOLATIONS OF BOURBON

Appalled at our four-year charade
"too few," "not at all," counting
the hours before I leave
the sword-points of your eyes
locked in our double jail's
"too few, not at all."

I want to leave you doors
that close when they don't open
the house I erected for my bird friends
the pasture where you dropped
the lazy silk of your behind
and I fondled it, "too few, not at all."
I want to stop my sink to your despair
to clench my hand, close-fisted, again
to sheathe my every wind and bone
in the crying banks of a night where I yaw
helm grinding in the green sand.

But wanting is not what I am,
a stick desiring a hen to clobber
a raincloud to burst in that dripping wilderness
where I first took you to my breast
and the stars murmured and the rain descended.

WRITTEN ON WATER

Bring ice that's always on fire,
bring your face, too. I need that,
your eyes especially, their wind
that invites noon's wildfires, their cry
that denudes yesterday's grass.

Bring your mouth, the palpable
greed invading each famished pore
whose inner longitude opens
onto battlements of clinging arms,
fields of windswept bone and skin.

Teach me to score the flakes
that vanish in carpeted snow;
to not know "hand" from "mouth";
to sense how your eyes' sealed lids
illustrate my gravest strokes.

In a dream of hair fire subsides.
In a dream of fire the red knife
sings to where I traipse
through exploding funnels
of indelicate rain.

REUNION

On muddy Soldier's Field
as fifty astronomical years converge
to dance the night away
our blood-filled ranks and arrogant skies
revolve: whirling cadences
syncopate the night.

We withstand encircling gravity
by making light of age—
pauses within infinity's stare—
as our receding fragments,
bent with time, march
into late night's surprises:
honey in a glass,
rain sifting down.

ACKNOWLEDGMENTS

My first publisher, George Hitchcock, saw us all paddling our uniquely individual kayaks. Optimistic, that. An art form in which no poem is ever truly finished tends to be more collaborative. I would never have gotten my own personal vessel down in the water, much less set it careening, but for my uncle James Merrill's lifelong encouragement. My wife, Juliet Mattila, has had a hand in nearly everything I've penned since. *Lifelines* has benefitted greatly from the incisive readings given by Lorrie and Barry Goldensohn.

The hypnagogic sequence, "Between Wake and Sleep," was a New Feral Press booklet, with collages by John Digby. Various bird poems were collected in "The Aviary," with collages again by John Digby.

BIOGRAPHICAL NOTE

Born 1936 in New York City, Robin Magowan received a BA from Harvard, MA from Columbia, and a PhD in comparative literature from Yale. During the 1960s, he taught at the University of Washington and the University of California at Berkeley. He moved to France in 1973, then to England in 1978, where in 1986 he founded the transatlantic review *Margin*, which he edited until 1990. The author of ten books of poetry, Magowan has also published a translation of Michaux's *Ecuador*; a study of the modern pastoral narrative, *Narcissus and Orpheus*; two collections of travel writing, *And Other Voyages* and *Fabled Cities: Samarkand, Bukhara, Khiva*; and two books on bicycle racing. He currently lives in Santa Fe, New Mexico where he copes with a large rock garden.

Printed in the USA
CPSIA information can be obtained
at www.ICGtesting.com
JSHW081108301123
52886JS00005B/111